Best Start

MUSIC LESSONS

SONG BOOK 1

for
Recorder
Fife
Flute

by Sarah Broughton Stalbow

Best Start Publishing
www.beststartmusic.com

First published in 2019 by Best Start Publishing

© Sarah Broughton Stalbow, 2019

ISBN: 978-0-6484270-8-7

All musical compositions by Sarah Broughton Stalbow, except for the following by Jeremy Barnett: *The Cake*, *Who's the boss?*, *At the Disco*, *The Dance*, *Mr Mouse*.

Cover art and text design by Sarah Broughton Stalbow, editing by Rob Stalbow.

A catalogue record for this book is available from the National Library of Australia

Best Start Publishing
www.beststartmusic.com

Audio tracks for songs are available at:

www.beststartmusic.com/backingtracks

Every song has a short instrumental introduction.

Stream them for free anytime and play along!

Piano accompaniments for songs 1 to 16 are available in the Best Start Music Lessons Book 1: For Teachers.

Piano accompaniments for songs 21 and 22 are available in Best Start Music Lessons Book 2: For Teachers.

Available from **www.beststartmusic.com** and on Amazon.

Remember to always:

Clap Sing Play

First: clap the rhythm.
Next: sing the note names.
Then: play it!

Reading Music

Music notes are written on 5 lines and 4 spaces - this is called the STAFF or STAVE.

You can remember the names of the notes on the LINES like this:

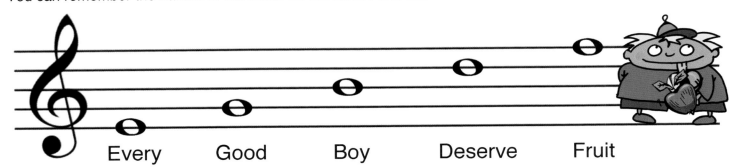

Every   Good   Boy   Deserve   Fruit

You can remember the notes in the SPACES like this:

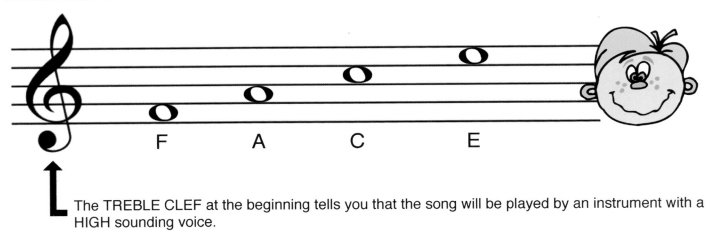

F   A   C   E

The TREBLE CLEF at the beginning tells you that the song will be played by an instrument with a HIGH sounding voice.

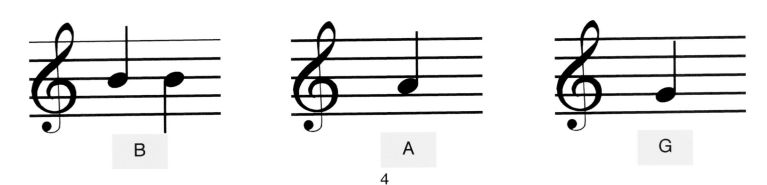

B   A   G

Reading Rhythms:

Symbol	Rhythm name	Notation name	Value
♩	Ta	Crotchet or Quarter Note	1 beat
♩	Ta-a	Minim or Half Note	2 beats
♩.	Ta-a-a	Dotted Minim or Dotted Half Note	3 beats
o	Great Big Whole Note	Semibreve or Whole Note	4 beats
♫	Ti-ti (Tee-tee)	Quavers or Eighth Notes	1/2 a beat each (together make one beat)

Clap these rhythms:

The TIME SIGNATURE tells you how many beats are in each bar.

Music is divided up into BARS by BARLINES.

Two dots at the end mean REPEAT.

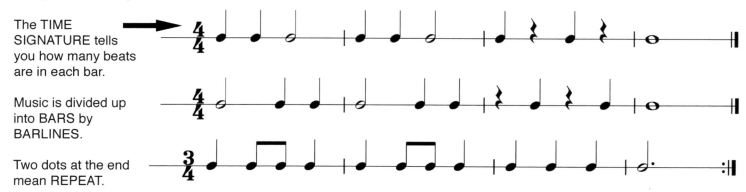

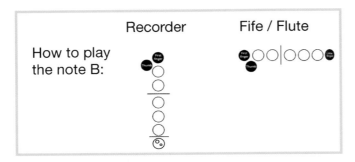

How to play the note B:

Recorder   Fife / Flute

1. Twinkle Star

Sing the first line of words (out loud or in your head),
then play the notes that follow.
Repeat for the following lines.

Twinkle twinkle little star

How I wonder what you are

Up above the world so high,
Like a diamond in the sky,
Twinkle twinkle little star

Up above the world so high,
Like a diamond in the sky,
Twinkle twinkle little star

2. Trick or Treat

Say: "B is fine on the middle line"

Point to the treble clef?

Try stamping your foot in the rests.

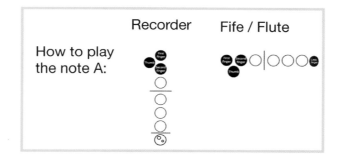

Recorder   Fife / Flute

How to play the note A:

3. The Spell

Say: "A sits in the second space"

How many As are in this song?

Optional lyrics:
Bubble bath and glitter glue,
Make this spell come true!

4. The Cake

Say: "B is fine on the middle line"
   "A sits in the second space"

Mixing mixing bake,
Icing icing cake,
Decorate,
Don't be late,
For some cake!

Point to the TIME SIGNATURE.

What does a 4 on the top mean?

5. Who's the boss?

Say: "G goes around the second line"

How many Gs are in this song?

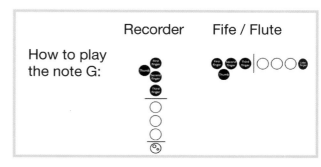

Recorder | Fife / Flute
How to play the note G:

6. Going to the Beach

7. At the Disco

Look carefully at at the music.
Point to the bars that are exactly the same.

8. Hide and Seek

10

9. The Dance

Step hop kick left,
Step hop kick right,
Sway to the left,
Sway to the right.

Point to the TIME SIGNATURE.

What does a number 3 on the top mean?

10. Dressing Up

What do the two dots at the end mean?

11

11. Super Snail

How many Bs are in this song?
How many As?

12. Mister Mouse

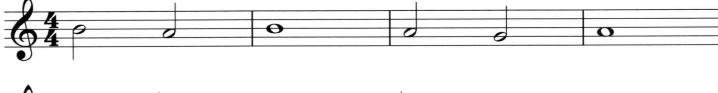

12

13. Waltz

14. Yo-yo

Sing the note names.

Which fingers move up and down together to play these notes?

15. Shake Your Hips!

Point to the quavers (eighth notes), then clap the rhythm.

16. Sparkle and Shine

17. Hot Cross Buns

| V | *This is a breath mark, take a breath here.* |

Teacher part:

18. Mary had a little lamb

Teacher part:

19. Roundabout

Teacher part:

20. Jump Up

Teacher part:

21. Icicles

Legato - smoothly

Wait for the 4 bar introduction, then play

22. Vámonos! *(Let's go!)*

Wait for the 4 bar introduction, then play

*Wait for the instrumental break,
then play it again!*

Stickers

CPSIA information can be obtained
at www.ICGtesting.com
Printed in the USA
LVIC060922160420
653686LV00001B/9